# GHANA

### COUNTRY EXPLORERS

Lyn Larson

Lerner Publications Company • Minneapolis

Lerner Publications Company
A division of Lerner Publishing Group, Inc.
241 First Avenue North
Minneapolis, MN 55401 USA

For reading levels and more information, look up this title at www.lernerbooks.com.


Library of Congress Cataloging-in-Publication Data

Larson, Lyn.
    Ghana / by Lyn Larson.
      p.   cm. — (Country explorers)
    Includes index.
    ISBN 978–0–7613–5318–8 (lib. bdg. : alk. paper)
    ISBN 978–0–7613–6249–4 (eBook)
    1. Ghana—Juvenile literature.  I. Title.
  DT510.L37  2011
  966.7—dc22                  2009048751

Manufactured in the United States of America
2 – PC – 11/1/13

# Table of Contents

# Welcome!

We're going to Ghana! Ghana is on the continent of Africa. The country is about 400 miles (644 kilometers) north of the equator.

Three countries lie along Ghana's borders. The Ivory Coast is to the west. Burkina Faso is to the north. And Togo is to the east. The Gulf of Guinea forms Ghana's southern border. Beyond the gulf is the Atlantic Ocean.

equator

Ghana

Fishing canoes dot a beach along the Gulf of Guinea.

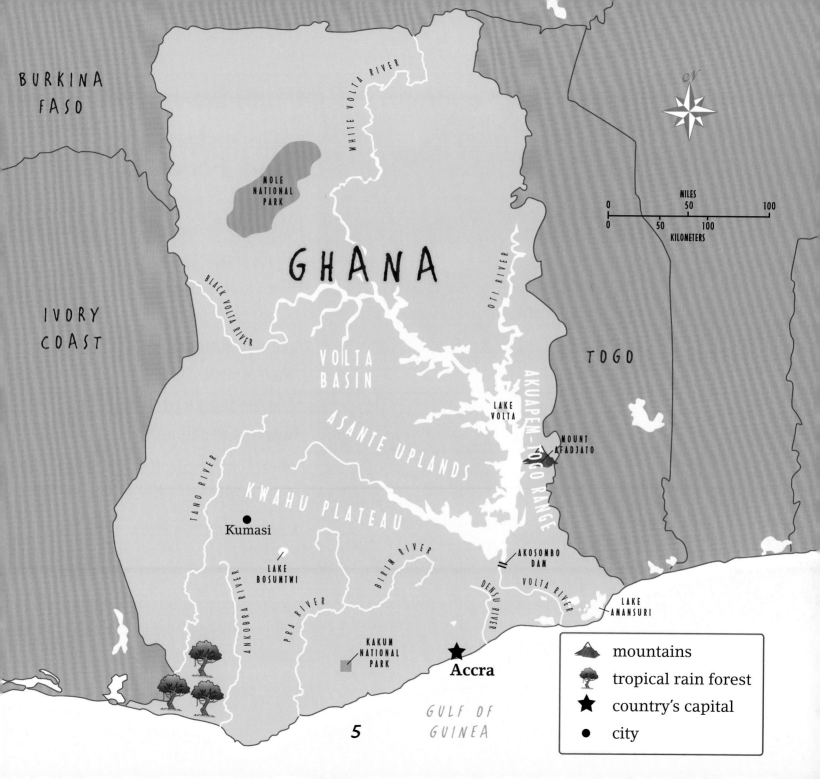

BURKINA
FASO

IVORY
COAST

*WHITE VOLTA RIVER*

GHANA

MOLE
NATIONAL
PARK

*BLACK VOLTA RIVER*

*OTI RIVER*

VOLTA
BASIN

TOGO

ASANTE UPLANDS

LAKE
VOLTA

*AKUAPEM-TOGO RANGE*

MOUNT
AFADJATO

*TANO RIVER*

KWAHU PLATEAU

● Kumasi

LAKE
BOSUMTWI

*BIRIM RIVER*

AKOSOMBO
DAM

*ANKOBRA RIVER*

*PRA RIVER*

*DENSU RIVER*

*VOLTA RIVER*

LAKE
AMANSURI

KAKUM
NATIONAL
PARK

★ **Accra**

*GULF OF
GUINEA*

5

| | |
|---|---|
| 🏔 | mountains |
| 🌳 | tropical rain forest |
| ★ | country's capital |
| ● | city |

## Grasslands and Forests

The land in northern Ghana is a savanna. That's a grassy plain. The weather there is hot and dry. A plateau runs across the country. This high, flat area separates the savanna in the north from the forests in the south.

Dry grasses blow in the winds on Ghana's savanna. A few scrubby trees add a dash of green.

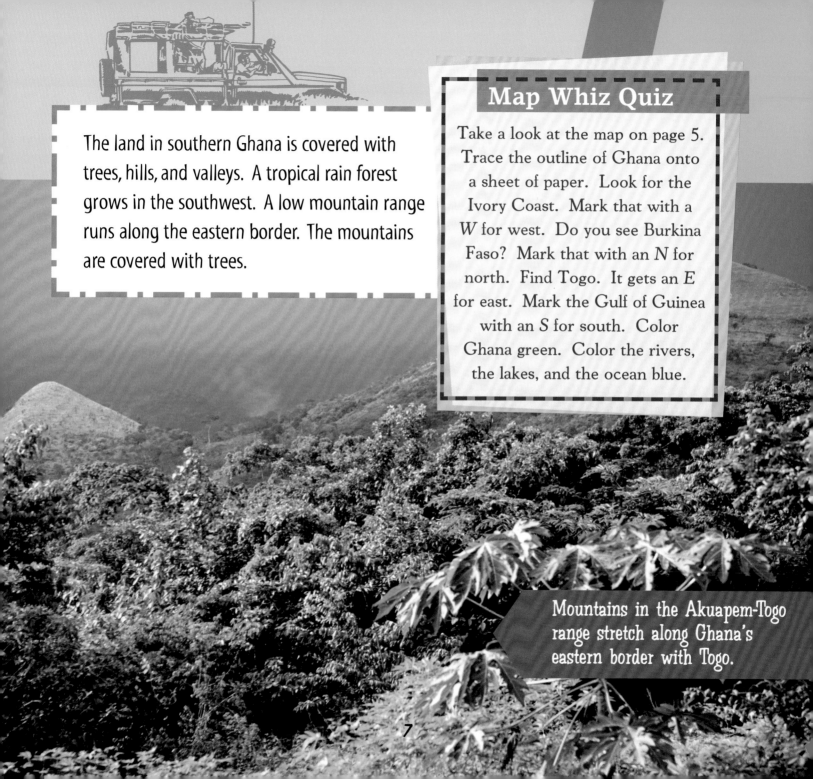

The land in southern Ghana is covered with trees, hills, and valleys. A tropical rain forest grows in the southwest. A low mountain range runs along the eastern border. The mountains are covered with trees.

Mountains in the Akuapem-Togo range stretch along Ghana's eastern border with Togo.

## Rivers and Lakes

Three long rivers cross northern Ghana. They are the Black Volta, the White Volta, and the Oti. These rivers all flow into the Volta River. In the 1960s, people built a dam on this river. The dam makes electricity. It also created Lake Volta. This is the largest lake ever made by people.

A dugout canoe makes its way up the Volta River.

In southern Ghana, the main rivers are the Tano, the Ankobra, the Pra, the Birim, and the Densu. These rivers and the Volta all flow into the Gulf of Guinea. Lake Bosumtwi is Ghana's only natural lake.

Ghanaians hold Lake Bosumtwi sacred. People can ride only on tree trunks, called *padua*. They must be paddled by hand.

## Amazing Animals

Are you ready to see some animals? Ghana has sixteen wildlife parks. The parks are home to many endangered animals. You might see elephants, lions, and chimpanzees. More wildlife areas also protect hippos, crocodiles, monkeys, and other animals from hunters.

These African elephants are the world's largest land animals. Here they are at a watering hole in Mole National Park.

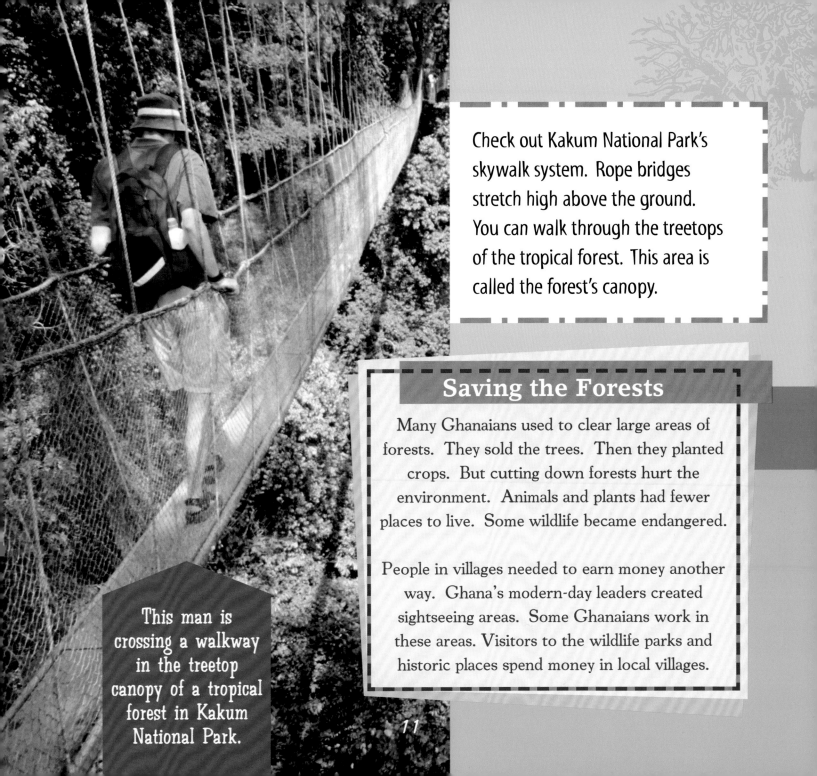

Check out Kakum National Park's skywalk system. Rope bridges stretch high above the ground. You can walk through the treetops of the tropical forest. This area is called the forest's canopy.

This man is crossing a walkway in the treetop canopy of a tropical forest in Kakum National Park.

## Saving the Forests

Many Ghanaians used to clear large areas of forests. They sold the trees. Then they planted crops. But cutting down forests hurt the environment. Animals and plants had fewer places to live. Some wildlife became endangered.

People in villages needed to earn money another way. Ghana's modern-day leaders created sightseeing areas. Some Ghanaians work in these areas. Visitors to the wildlife parks and historic places spend money in local villages.

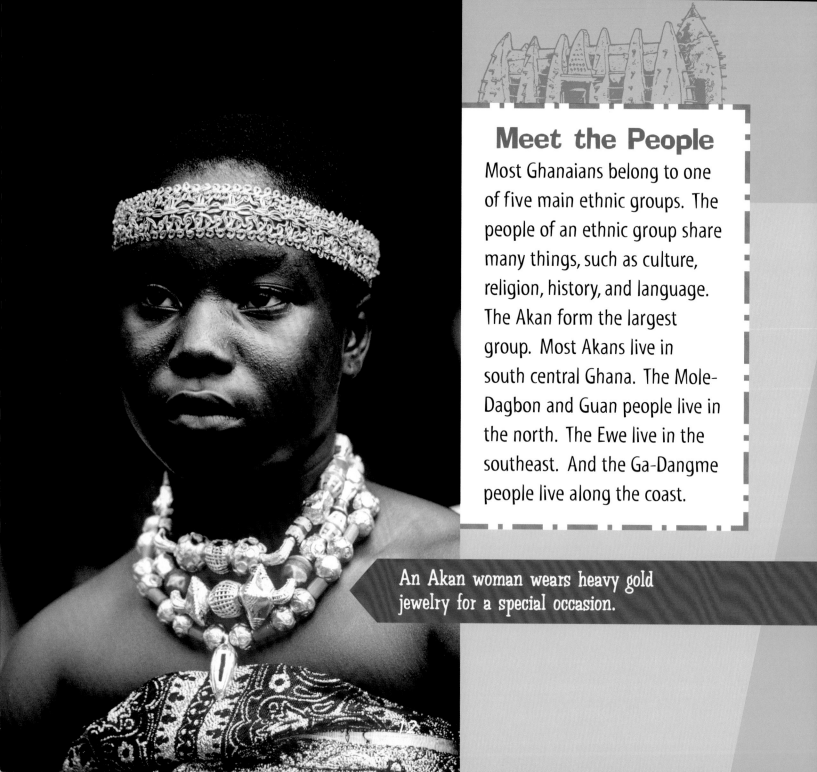

## Meet the People

Most Ghanaians belong to one of five main ethnic groups. The people of an ethnic group share many things, such as culture, religion, history, and language. The Akan form the largest group. Most Akans live in south central Ghana. The Mole-Dagbon and Guan people live in the north. The Ewe live in the southeast. And the Ga-Dangme people live along the coast.

An Akan woman wears heavy gold jewelry for a special occasion.

12

The Asante people are part of the Akan group. In the 1600s, the Asante had a powerful kingdom in western Africa. The city of Kumasi was its cultural center. Many Asante still live in this part of central Ghana.

A group of young Asante boys pose playfully for a photo.

# The Gold Coast

What's that shiny metal? It's gold! Rich deposits of gold lie in south central Ghana. In ancient times, western African chiefs had jewelry and other objects made of gold. People used gold as we use money. They traded gold for goods they wanted to buy.

This man is holding a small piece of gold that he found on a mining site.

Other countries also wanted Ghana's gold. In the 1400s, people from Europe sailed to western Africa. The Europeans called this region the Gold Coast. They traded cloth and other goods for gold. Soon the Europeans built forts and castles as trading posts.

## The Golden Stool

In the 1600s, the Asante chief was Osei Tutu. He united many Akan tribes under his rule. A golden stool was his sign of power. Legend says the stool floated down from the sky. The Asante protected the stool. They believed they would lose control of their kingdom if it was stolen. The Golden Stool is still a sign of power.

Europeans built Elmina Castle between 1471 and 1482. This castle was the first one that Europeans built south of the Sahara in northern Africa.

15

Slave traders tied both children and adults by their necks and wrists as they walked in a chain. A guard with a gun walked beside them.

## Slave Trade

In the 1500s, European traders began taking people as slaves in western Africa. Slaves were unpaid workers. They had no freedom. The slave traders sold the African slaves to white people in North America and South America. White owners forced slaves to work on farms or in houses.

The slave trade ended in the mid-1800s. Many Europeans left western Africa. But Great Britain wanted to make the Gold Coast a colony. The British army attacked the Asante kingdom. They fought many battles. Finally, the British defeated the Asante in 1901. The British also took control of other areas along the coast and in the north.

A troop of British soldiers attack a group of Asante in western Africa during a battle in the 1870s.

# Freedom!

The British controlled the Gold Coast for fifty-five years. They had African workers build roads, railways, and harbors. The British started large mining companies. And the British brought new crops, such as the cacao tree. Britain benefited from the country's wealth. But the Ghanaian people did not.

African workers peel the fruit of cacao trees. The fruit is used to make chocolate.

Africans wanted to rule themselves. They demanded rights. In 1952, the British made Kwame Nkrumah the top African leader in the colony. Other leaders wrote a constitution. On March 6, 1957, British control ended. Ghana became an independent country.

## Naming Ghana

The new country of Ghana took its name from an ancient kingdom. Ancient Ghana was the first great kingdom in western Africa. The kingdom was a center of trade for hundreds of years. But it was farther north and west. Over time, people from this kingdom may have moved into the area that became modern-day Ghana.

Kwame Nkrumah, the first Ghanaian head of government, arrives in the capital city of Accra to lead the newly independent country.

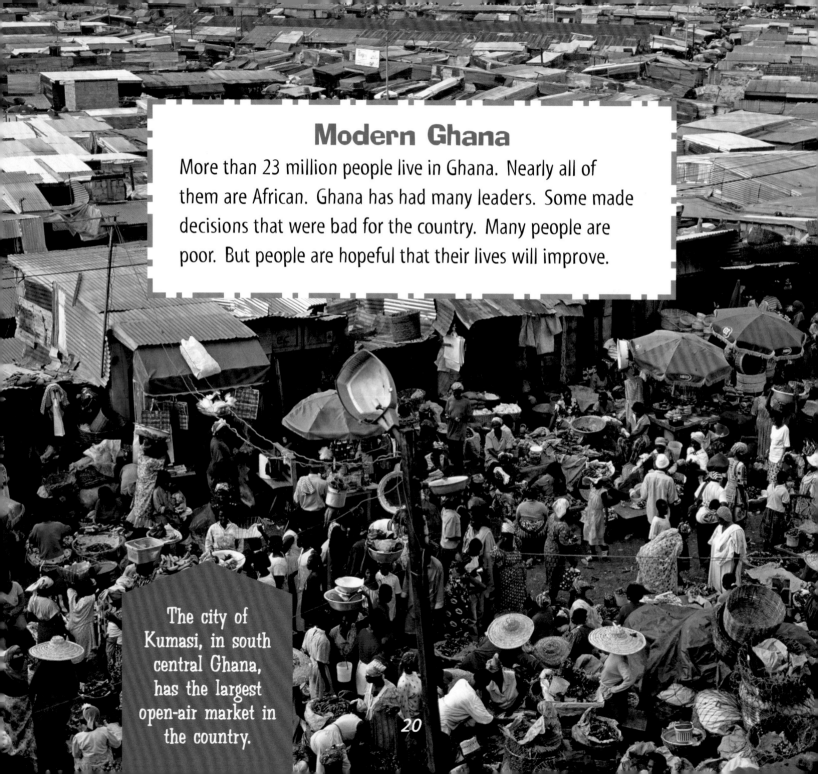

## Modern Ghana

More than 23 million people live in Ghana. Nearly all of them are African. Ghana has had many leaders. Some made decisions that were bad for the country. Many people are poor. But people are hopeful that their lives will improve.

The city of Kumasi, in south central Ghana, has the largest open-air market in the country.

20

How do people in Ghana earn a living? Many people are farmers. Ghana is the second-largest producer of cacao beans in the world. Other farm crops include rice, cassava, peanuts, corn, and bananas. Many people also work in the lumber business, in factories, as fishers, and in tourism.

## Oil!

In 2007, a British company discovered oil near the coast of Ghana. Oil is sometimes called black gold. Oil wells started pumping in 2010. The discovery of oil creates jobs. It will bring more money into the country.

Seeds from the pods of cacao trees are dried before they can be roasted. Each pod holds twenty to forty seeds.

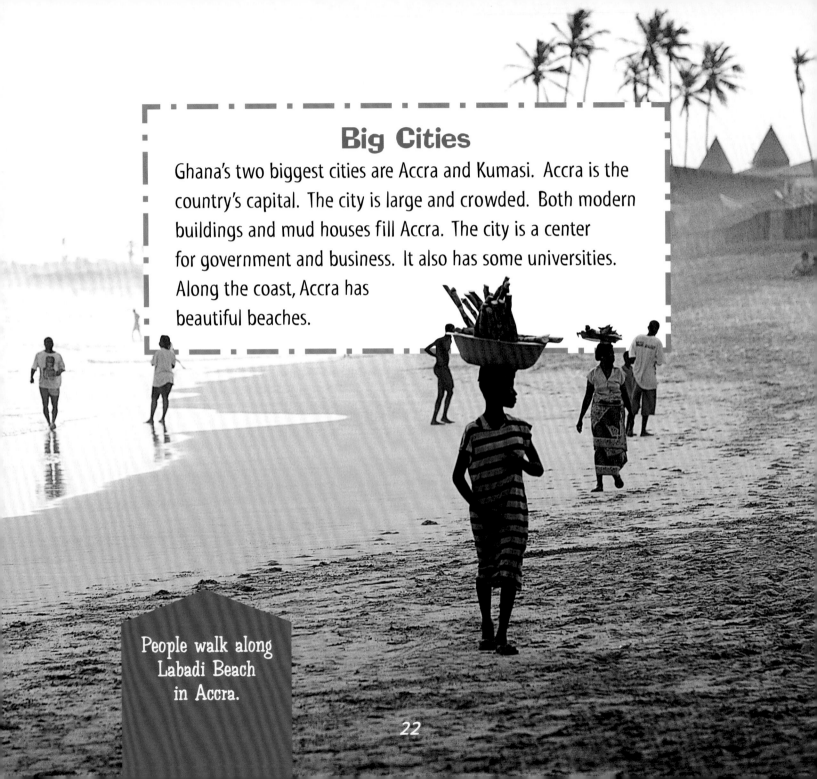

## Big Cities

Ghana's two biggest cities are Accra and Kumasi. Accra is the country's capital. The city is large and crowded. Both modern buildings and mud houses fill Accra. The city is a center for government and business. It also has some universities. Along the coast, Accra has beautiful beaches.

People walk along Labadi Beach in Accra.

Kumasi is Ghana's second-largest city. The city is still an important center for the Asante people. Many museums display historic Asante items. Kumasi also has one of the largest outdoor markets in western Africa. Thousands of people sell their goods there.

## President Obama Visits Accra

In July 2009, U.S. president Barack Obama visited Ghana. The president made a speech in Accra. He said, "Ghana's history is rich [and] the ties between our two countries are strong." He encouraged Ghana's leaders to make good decisions for their country.

President Barack Obama spoke to members of the Ghanaian government in Accra in 2009.

# Village Life

Most Ghanaians live in villages in the countryside. Many people are farmers. They grow crops and raise small animals such as chickens. Some northern families also have cattle. Most people living near the coast, the lakes, and the rivers are fishers.

The walls of this building are made of mud. The house has a roof made of bundles of grass.

Family members often live together in small villages. People share outside areas for cooking and eating together. Some villages have wells for people to get water. In other areas, people carry water from rivers or lakes. Larger villages might have a church or other places of worship, a school, a clinic, and other buildings.

Women serve lunch to schoolchildren in a village in northern Ghana.

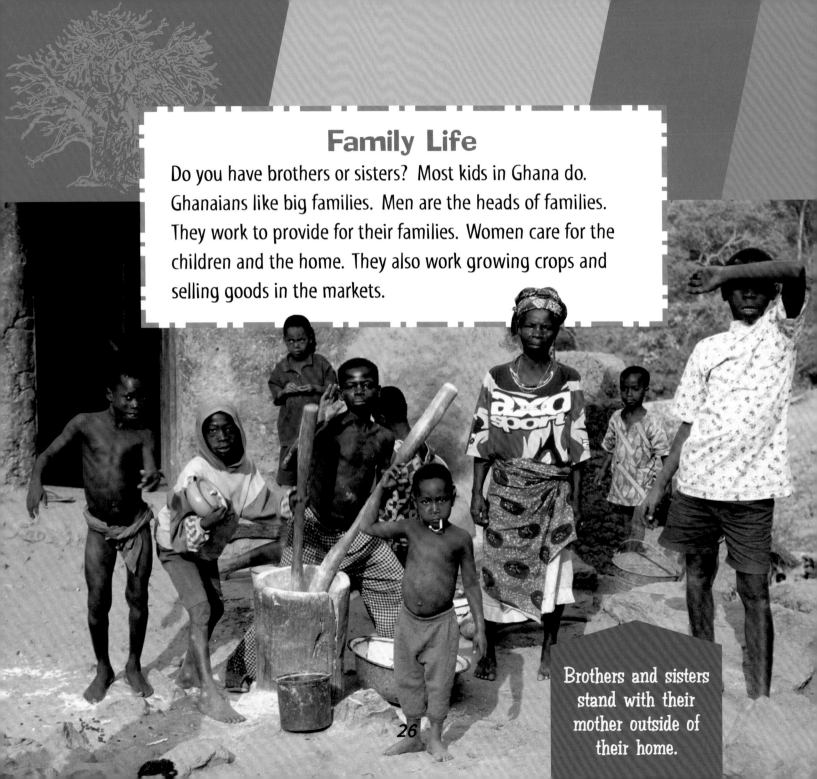

# Family Life

Do you have brothers or sisters? Most kids in Ghana do. Ghanaians like big families. Men are the heads of families. They work to provide for their families. Women care for the children and the home. They also work growing crops and selling goods in the markets.

Brothers and sisters stand with their mother outside of their home.

26

In the countryside, many families live in mud homes. Other homes have concrete walls with tin roofs. Most families grow their own food. In big cities, many families live in apartment buildings or small houses. Most men and some women have jobs. City families mainly buy their food at markets.

Family members gather outside their home in Accra.

# Getting Around

Ghana has roads that connect many big cities. Some people own cars or trucks. Many people take buses, taxis, or *tro-tros*. Tro-tros are small buses or trucks. People pay to ride on them. Tro-tros don't come and go at regular times. Drivers leave only when all the seats are full.

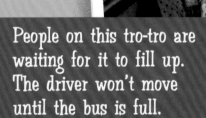

People on this tro-tro are waiting for it to fill up. The driver won't move until the bus is full.

Ghanaians also use rivers and lakes to get around. Some travel in flat-bottomed canoes and boats. On Lake Volta, ferries and cargo ships carry people and goods from city to city. Ghana also has twelve airports and a train system.

Canoes are the only way to get to and from some rural villages on Lake Amansuri.

## Schooltime

Kids in Ghana often go to school from the age of four to the age of nineteen. They study math, science, English, social studies, and art. In cities, many kids go to grade school until the age of twelve. They attend junior high for three years and senior high for four years. After high school, some students go on to universities. Others learn a trade.

Some villages don't have school buildings. Teachers hold classes outdoors. One teacher might cover many grades. In poorer areas, some kids don't go to school very often. They need to work to help their families.

Classes in this village grade school take place outdoors.

## Let's Eat!

Are you hungry? Some of the main foods in Ghana are yams, corn, and plantains. Plantains are a type of banana. For protein, people eat eggs, fish, beans, and peanuts.

This woman is making a sauce of tomatoes and vegetables for her family's dinner.

Ghanaians often make stews from vegetables and fish or meat. Many people eat *fufu* with their stew. Fufu is made with yams or cassava. Cooks peel, slice, and boil the vegetables. They mash them and then form them into balls. People dip the fufu into their stew.

## Still Hungry?

Here are some other common dishes in Ghana:

*oto*—mashed yams with eggs

*waakye*—spicy beans and rice

*bofrot*—fried doughnuts

*red-red*—fried plantains with bean stew

*kenkey*—dumplings made from cornmeal

Ghanian children eat balls of fufu from a shared bowl.

# Religions

Most Ghanaians are Christians. Many Christians live in the southern part of Ghana. In the north, many people are Muslims. They practice the religion of Islam.

Muslims leave a mosque (place of prayer) after Friday prayers. The mosque has mud walls. The walls must be repaired each year.

Some Ghanaians follow a religion based on nature. They believe in one powerful God and many lesser gods. The lesser gods might be animals, plants, or rocks. People ask these lesser gods for help. These Ghanaians also believe that dead family members watch over them.

This holy person leads a local service in Kumasi. This religion is closely linked to nature.

## Celebrate!

Are you ready for some fun? Ghanaians celebrate many events. For example, harvest festivals are held around the country. People enjoy watching drummers, singers, and dancers.

Drummers take part in Homowo, a harvest festival for the Ga-Dangme people living near Accra.

On March 6, the whole country celebrates Independence Day. Ghana won freedom from British control on this date in 1957. To celebrate, Ghanaians wear clothing with the colors of their country's flag—green, yellow, black, and red. Many cities have parades, music, and dancing.

Ghanaians celebrate Independence Day in Accra. Ghana was the first African country to win freedom from British rule.

## Art Treasures

Many people value the kente cloth that Asante and Ewe artists weave. Weavers make kente cloth with brightly colored thread. They make narrow strips of it on a loom. Then they sew the strips into larger pieces of cloth. The Asante also make Adinkra cloth. They stamp designs on a solid-colored cloth background.

Long ago, only kings could wear kente cloth. In the late 1900s, this brightly colored cloth became the national dress of Ghana.

Wood-carvers make dolls, masks, stools, and sculptures. Goldsmiths make beautiful jewelry. Other special Ghanaian crafts include brass figures, clay pottery, glass beads, and woven baskets.

Dear Mom and Dad,
We went to the Arts Center in Accra today. We saw people selling crafts from all parts of the country. The kente cloth is so colorful. The yellow, black, red, and green patterns reminded me of Ghana's flag. I also liked the wooden sculptures. One merchant showed us how people make drums. I had a great day!

See you soon!
Jeff

Accra, Ghana

The National Cultural Center in Accra sells Ghanaian arts and crafts such as these.

# Dance and Music

Local Ghanaian dances often tell stories. The Ewe have a dance about how their people used to live in another country. They followed a bird to their new home in Ghana. Drummers play music for the dances. Sometimes players use flutes and other instruments too.

Local people in eastern Ghana dance to the music of drummers.

Newer styles of music combine African sounds with other music. Highlife music started in Ghana in the 1920s. It blends local music with European hymns and military songs. In the 1990s, Ghanaians started to mix highlife music with American hip-hop. They call this new music hiplife.

## Talking Drums

Specially shaped drums can sound like the Asante language. Players squeeze cords along the side of the drum. This changes the drum's sound. The drums sound as if someone is talking. The Asante once used these drums to send messages between villages.

This lively crowd is enjoying a hiplife concert on Labadi Beach in Accra.

41

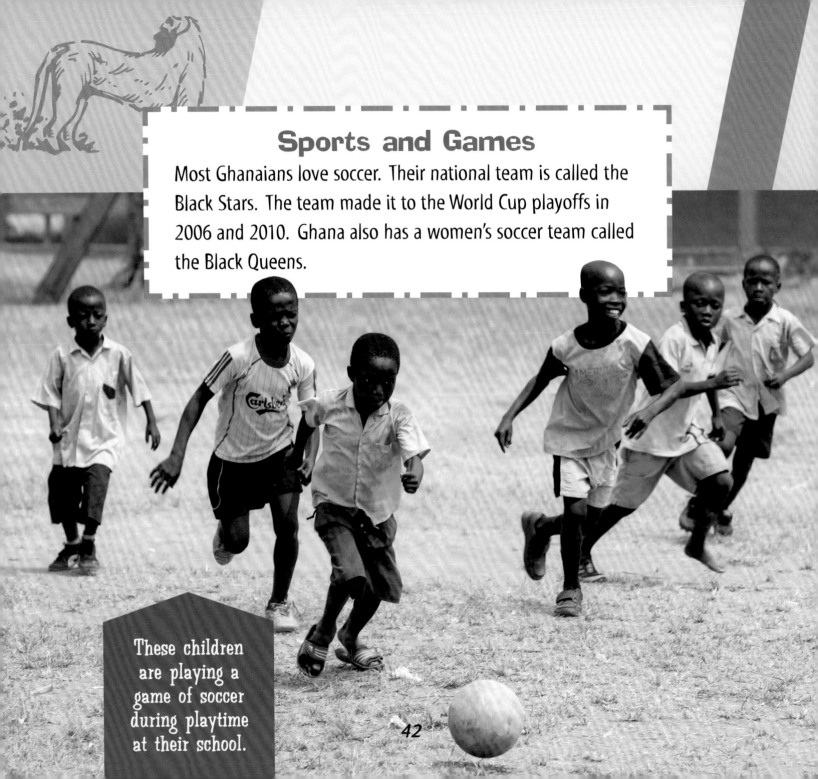

# Sports and Games

Most Ghanaians love soccer. Their national team is called the Black Stars. The team made it to the World Cup playoffs in 2006 and 2010. Ghana also has a women's soccer team called the Black Queens.

These children are playing a game of soccer during playtime at their school.

42

An exciting oware
game keeps the
interest of this family.

Kids and adults also enjoy the board game *oware*. Players use
a wooden board with two rows of cups in it. They use markers
such as seeds or small stones. The players take turns. Each player
picks up markers in a certain order. The player who collects all the
markers wins the game. Oware is one of the world's oldest games.

## THE FLAG OF GHANA

Ghana's flag has three stripes. The bottom one is green. It stands for the country's forests and farms. The middle stripe is golden shade of yellow. It stands for the country's mineral wealth. The top stripe is red. It stands for those who died while fighting for Ghana's independence. A black star is in the center. It stands for freedom.

## FAST FACTS

FULL COUNTRY NAME: Republic of Ghana

AREA: 92,100 square miles (238,537 square kilometers), or about the same size as Oregon

MAIN LANDFORMS: the Kwahu Plateau; the Asante Uplands; the Volta Basin; the mountain range Akuapem-Togo; the savanna; tropical rain forests

MAJOR RIVERS: Volta (formed by the White Volta, Black Volta, and Oti), Tano, Ankobra, Pra, Birim, and Densu

ANIMALS AND THEIR HABITATS: African elephants, lions, hyenas, aardvarks, roan antelopes, and vultures (mainly savanna); forest elephants and leopards (mainly forests); chimpanzees (rain forests); warthogs (savanna, forests, and rain forests); crocodiles, hippos, and manatees (rivers and lakes); marine turtles (ocean); rock pythons and black mamba snakes (widespread)

CAPITAL CITY: Accra

OFFICIAL LANGUAGE: English

POPULATION: about 23,832,495

# GLOSSARY

**cacao bean:** a bean that grows in the fruit of cacao trees. It is used to make chocolate.

**canopy:** the top layer of the rain forest, formed by branches of the trees

**capital:** a city where the government of a state or country is located

**cassava:** a root vegetable that can be boiled or ground into flour

**colony:** a territory controlled by the government of another country

**continent:** any one of Earth's seven large areas of land. The continents are Africa, Antarctica, Asia, Australia, Europe, North America, and South America.

**endangered:** in danger of dying off completely

**ethnic group:** a group of people that shares many things in common, such as customs, religion, history, and language

**gulf:** a part of an ocean that reaches into land

**map:** a drawing or chart of all or part of Earth or the sky

**mosque:** an Islamic place of worship

**mountain:** a part of Earth's surface that rises high into the sky

**plateau:** a large area of high, level land

**savanna:** a dry, grassy, flatland

**tourism:** traveling and visiting places for pleasure

**tropical rain forest:** a thick, green forest that gets lots of rain every year

## TO LEARN MORE

### BOOKS

Blauer, Ettagle. *Ghana*. New York: Children's Press, 2009. Discover more about Ghana's history and culture.

Garner, Lynne. *African Crafts: Fun Things to Make and Do from West Africa*. Chicago: Chicago Review Press, 2004. Learn about and make crafts from Ghana and other parts of western Africa.

Krensky, Stephen. *Anansi and the Box of Stories: A West African Folktale*. Minneapolis: Millbrook Press, 2008. Find out how Anansi wins the sky god's box of stories.

McNamara, Catherine. *Nii Kwei's Day: From Dawn to Dusk in a Ghanaian City*. Child's Day series. London: Frances Lincoln Childrens Books, 2003. Meet Nii Kwei and follow him through his day.

Milway, Katie Smith. *One Hen—How One Small Loan Made a Big Difference*. Toronto: Kids Can Press, 2008. Kojo's family borrows money from a community bank to buy a hen. The hen's eggs feed his family, and some are left over to sell. See what happens with just one hen.

### WEBSITES

**Africa for Kids**
http://pbskids.org/africa/
See what life is like for some kids living in Accra, Ghana. You can also play a thumb piano, make an African mask, and learn more about other countries in Africa.

**Enchanted Learning**
http://enchanted learning.com
Find a map of Ghana, a map quiz, the flag of Ghana, and more at this site.

## INDEX